Al-Hariri Assemblies
(Maqamat al-Hariri)

Editors
Sheila Summerfield
Hasan Yahya

@ DYTV Volcano Publisher-2012

ISBN-13: 978-1470050634
ISBN-10: 1470050633

Manufactured in the United States of America

Content

Introduction		04
Al-Hariri Introduction		10
Assembly (Maqamah)	No. 01	17
Assembly (Maqamah)	No. 02	23
Assembly (Maqamah)	No. 03	30
Assemby (Maqamah)	No. 04	36
Assembly (Maqamah)	No. 05	43
Assembly (Maqamah)	No. 06	51
Assembly (Maqamah)	No. 07	60
Assemby (Maqamah)	No. 08	67
Assembly (Maqamah)	No 09	74
Assembly (Maqamah)	No. 10	83
Assembly (Maqamah)	No. 11	90
Assemby (Maqamah)	No. 12	97

Sources	106
About the Editors	108

Introduction:

One of al-Hariri's contemporaries, the famous Zamakhshari, has expressed the general verdict in pithy verse:

"I swear by God and His marvels,
By pilgrims' rite and their shrine:
Hariri's Assemblies are worthy
To be wrotten in gold each line.

Al-Maqamat was originated as an art by Badi al-Zaman al-Hamadani, who died in the eighth year after the first millennium (1008).

He was credited with inventing the genre known as *maqamat* ("assemblies") - dramatic anecdotes narrated by a witty but unscrupulous rogue which poke fun at all levels of society. Elaborately written in rhyming prose, they exploit the unique capabilities of the Arabic language to the full. Out of 400 original *maqamat,* 52 survive. The trend towards linguistic virtuosity led, ultimately, to a triumph of form over content. al-hariri (c 1054-1122) took the *maqamah* to new heights (or extremes) in order to demonstrate his prowess with word-play and his seemingly inexhaustible vocabulary. In one work, he used only those letters of the alphabet which have no dots or do not join to the following letter in a word. Even so, for more than seven centuries, al-Hariri's *maqamat* were regarded as the greatest literary treasure of Arabic, after the Qur'an. According to some readers, wholesome moral values and subtle criticisms of the existing social order underlie al-Hariri's decorative language. This book includes 12 of al-Hariri Assemblies.

Maqamat Al Hariri in Arab Literature was famous asan art through Al -Hariri (446-516 A.H./1054-1122): *Maqamat* means *Assemblies.*

Pure entertainment for the masses as well as for more sophisticated audience formed an important part of the adab (non-religious, entertainment) literature. The two outstanding examples of works addressed to the latter were the socalled maqamat, a literary term usually translated as "assemblies" or "séances." Full of wit and learned allusions, they presupposed a knowledgeable audience that could appreciate them. The creator of this art form - for it was art and not instruction that the author had in mind - was Badi' al-Zamdn, "Wonder of the Age," al-Hamadhdni (359-99 A.H./969-1008 A.D.). The leading character of his work was Abu'l-Fatih of Alexandria, the wandering scholar, the Muslim counterpart of the Fahrende Schüler or Vagans Clericus of medieval Europe, who lived by his wits roving through the land. The narrator of the Maqamat pretends to have encountered this character wherever he went and entertained his audience with Abu'l-Fatih's erudition and the anecdotes he told.

The Maqamat were composed in a style characteristic for this art form, They were cast into the ancient form of saj, "rhymed prose" (the form, as will be remembered, in which the Koran was revealed). Each maqamat dealt with a separate topic, the whole being unified by the persons of the narrator and the traveler, Abu'lFatb in al-Hamadhani's Maqamat, Abu Zayd of Saruj in those by the later al-Hariri (446-516 A.H./1054-1122 A.D.), This style enabled the authors to display all the brilliancy of their erudition, their rhetoric, and their wit. The maqdmdt became almost the best known and most highly appreciated literary works of

6

later times among the Arabs; in particular, al-Hariri's Maqamat were praised highly and remained a favorite in the Muslim world. They found imitators all over its sphere of influence, including, in Spain, the Maadmat of the Jewish thinker al-Harizi (thirteenth century).

Excerpted from Philip Hitti, History of the Arabs, 10th ed. (London: Macmillan, 1970)

Arabic literature in the narrow sense of adab (belles-lettres) began with al-Jahiz (d. 868-9), the sheikh of the Bazrah littérateurs, and reached its culmination in the fourth and fifth Moslem centuries in the works of Badi al-Zaman al-Hamadhani (969-1008), al-Tha'alibi of Naysabur (961-1038) and al-Hariri (1054-1122). One characteristic feature of prose-writing in this period was the tendency, in response to Persian influence, to be affected and ornate. The terse, incisive and simple expression of early days had gone for ever. It was supplanted by polished and elegant style, rich in elaborate similes and replete with rhymes. The whole period was marked by a predominance of humanistic over scientific studies. Intellectually it was a period of decline. It supported a literary proletariat, many of whose members, with no independent means of livelihood, roamed from place to place ready to give battle over linguistic issues and grammatical technicalities or to measure poetical swords over trivial matters with a view to winning favours from wealthy patrons. This .period also saw the rise of a new form of literary expression, the maqamah.

Badi al-Zaman ("wonder of the age") al-Hamadhani is credited with the creation of the maqdamah (assembly), a kind of dramatic anecdote in the telling of which the author subordinates substance to form and does his utmost to display his poetical ability, learning and eloquence. In reality such a form of composition as the maqdmah could not have been the creation of any one man; it was a natural development of rhymed prose and flowery diction as represented by ibn-Durayd and earlier stylists. Al-Hamadhani's work 2 served as a model for al-Hariri of al-Basrah, whose Maqamat for more than seven centuries were esteemed as the chief treasure, next to the Koran, of the literary Arabic tongue. In these maqamat of al-Hariri and other writers there is much more than the elegant form and rhetorical anecdote which most readers consider the only significant feature. The anecdote itself is often used as a subtle and indirect way of criticizing the existing social order and drawing a wholesome moral. Since the days of al-Hamadhani and al-ljariri the maqdmah has become the most perfect form of literary and dramatic presentation in Arabic, a language which has never produced real drama.

Excerpted from Ilse Lichtenstadter, Introduction to Classical Arabic Literature, *(Boston: Twayne, 1974), p. 122*

Introduction by al-Hariri

O God, we praise thee for what perspicuity thou hast taught, and what enunciation thou hast inspired; as we praise thee for what bounty thou hast enlarged, what mercy thou hast diffused: And we take refuge with thee from the vehemence of fluency and the immoderation of talkativeness, as we take refuge with thee from the vice of inarticulateness and the shame of hesitation. And by thee we seek to be kept from temptation through the flattery of the praiser and the connivance of the favor, as we seek to be kept from exposure to the defaming of the slanderer and the betrayal of the informer. And we ask pardon of thee if our desires carry us into the region of ambiguities, as we ask pardon if our steps advance to the domain of errors. And we ask of thee succor which shall lead us aright, and a heart turning with justice, and a tongue adorned with truth, and a speech strengthened with demonstration, and accuracy that shall keep us from mistake, and resolution that shall conquer caprice, and perception by which we may estimate duly: And that thou wilt help us by thy guidance to conceive, and enable us by thy assistance to express; that thou wilt guard us from error in narration, and turn us from unseemliness in jesting; that we may be secure from slanders of the tongue; that we may be free from the ill of tinseled speech; that we walk not in the road of sin, nor stand in the place of repentance; that we be not pursued by suit or censure, nor need to flee from hastiness to excuse. O God, fulfil to us this wish; give us to attain to this desire: put us not forth of thy large shadow, make us not a morsel for the devourer. For now we stretch forth to thee the hand of entreaty; we are thorough in humiliation to thee and abasement. And we call down thy abundant grace and thy bounty that is over all, with humbleness of seeking and with the venture of hope. Also approaching thee through the merits of Mohammed, lord of men, the intercessor whose intercession shall be received at the congregation of judgment. By whom thou hast set the seal to the prophets, and whose degree thou hast exalted to the highest heaven; whom thou hast described in thy clear-speaking Book, and hast said (and thou art the most truthful of sayers): "It is the word of a noble envoy, of him who is mighty in the presence of the tord of the throne, having authority, obeyed, yea, faithful." O God, send thy blessing on him and his house who guide aright, and his companions who built up the faith; and make us followers of his guidance and theirs, and profit us all by the loving of him and them: for thou art Almighty, and one meet to answer prayer.

And now: In a meeting devoted to that learning whose breeze has stilled in this age, whose lights are nigh gone out, there ran a mention of the Assemblies which had been invented by Badi'az Zeman, the sage of Hamadan (God show him mercy); in which he had referred the composition to Abu'l Fath of Alexandria and the relation of 'Isa, son of Hisham. And both these are persons obscure, not known; vague, not to be recognized. Then suggested to me one whose suggestion is as a decree, and obedience to whom is as a prize, that I should compose Assemblies, following in them the method of Badi' (although the lame steed attains not to outrun like the stout one). Then I reminded him of what is said concerning him who joins even two words, or strings together one or two verses: and deprecated this position in which the understanding is bewildered, and the fancy misses aim, and the depth of the intelligence is probed, and a man's real value is made manifest: and in which one is forced to be as a wood-gatherer by night, or as he who musters footmen and horsemen together: considering, too, that the voluble man is seldom secure or pardoned if he trips. But when he consented not to forbearance, and freed me not from his demand, I assented to his invitation with the assenting of the obedient, and displayed in according with him all my endeavor; and composed, in spite of what I suffered from frozen genius, and dimmed intelligence, and failing judgment, and afflicting cares, fifty Assemblies, comprising what is serious in language and lively, what is delicate in expression and dignified; the brilliancies of eloquence and its pearls, and beauties of scholarship and its rarities: besides what I have adorned them with of verses of the Qur'an and goodly metonymies, and studded them with of Arab proverbs, and scholarly elegancies, and grammatical riddles, and decisions dependent on the meaning of words, and original addresses, and ornate orations, and tear-moving exhortations, and amusing jests: all of which I have indited as by the tongue of Abu Zayd of Seruj, while I have attributed the relating of them to Al Harith, son of Hammam, of Basra. And whenever I change the pasture I have no purpose but to inspirit the reader, and to increase the number of those who shall seek my book. And of the poetry of others I have introduced nothing but two single verses, on which I have based the fabric of the Assembly of Holwan; and two others, in a couplet, which I have inserted at the conclusion of the Assembly of Kerej. And, as for the rest, my own mind is the father of its virginity, the author of its sweet and its bitter. Yet I acknowledge withal that Badi' (God show him mercy) is a mighty passer of goals, a worker of wonders; and that he who essays after him to the composition of an Assembly, even though he be gifted with the eloquence of Kodameh, does but scoop up of his overflow, and travels that path only by his guidance. And excellently said one:

If before it mourned, I had mourned my love for Su'da, then should I have healed my soul, nor had afterward to repent. But it mourned before me, and its mourning excited mine, and I said, " The superiority is to the one that is first."

Now I hope I shall not be, in respect of the playful style that I display, and the source that I repair to, like the beast that scratched up its death with its hoof, or he who cut off his nose with his own hand; so as to be joined to those who are "most of all losers in their works, whose course on earth has been in vain, while they count that they have done fair deeds." Since I know that although he who is intelligent and liberal will connive at me, and he who is friendly and partial may defend me, I can hardly escape from the simpleton who is ignorant, or the spiteful man who feigns ignorance; who will detract from me on account of this composition, and will give out that it is among the things forbidden of the law. But yet, whoever scans matters with the eye of intelligence, and makes good his insight into principles, will rank these Assemblies in the order of useful writings, and class them with the fables that relate to brutes and lifeless objects. Now none was ever heard of whose hearing shrank from such tales, or who held as sinful those who related them at ordinary times. Moreover, since deeds depend on intentions, and in these lies the effectiveness of religious obligations, what fault is there in one who composes stories for instruction, not for display, and whose purpose in them is the education and not the fablings? Nay, is he not in the position of one who assents to doctrine, and "guides to the right path"?

Yet am I content if I may carry my caprice, and then be quit of it, without any debt against me or to me.

And of God I seek to be helped in what I purpose, and to be kept from that which makes defective, and to be led to that which leads aright. For there is no refuge but to him, and no seeking of succor but in him, and no prospering but from him, and no sanctuary but he. On him I rely, and to him I have recourse.

Al-Hariri Assemblies in Arabic Literature

The First Assembly

Al Harith, son of Hammam, related: When I mounted the hump of exile, and misery removed me from my fellows, the shocks of the time cast me to San'a of Yemen. And I entered it with wallets empty, manifest in my need; I had not a meal; I found not in my sack a mouthful. Then began I to traverse its ways like one crazed, and to roam in its depths as roams the thirsting bird. And wherever ranged my glances, wherever ran my goings at morn or even, I sought some generous man before whom I might fray the tissue of my countenance, to whom I might be open concerning my need; or one well bred, whose aspect might dispel my pain, whose anecdote might relieve my thirsting. Until the close of my circuit brought me, and the overture of courtesy guided me, to a wide place of concourse, in which was a throng and a wailing. Then I entered the thicket of the crowd to explore what was drawing forth tears. And I saw in the middle of the ring a person slender of make; upon him was the equipment of pilgrimage, and he had the voice of lamentation. And he was studding cadences with the jewels of his wording, and striking hearings with the reproofs of his admonition.

And now the medley of the crowds had surrounded him, as the halo surrounds the moon, or the shell the fruit. So I crept toward him, that I might catch of his profitable sayings, and gather up of his gems. And I heard him say, as he coursed along in his career, and the throat of his improvisation made utterance:

O thou reckless in petulance, trailing the garment of vanity! O thou headstrong in follies, turning aside to idle tales! How long wilt thou persevere in thine error, and eat sweetly of the pasture of thy wrong? How far wilt thou be extreme in thy pride, and not abstain from thy wantonness? Thou provokest by thy rebellion the Master of thy forelock; in the foulness of thy behaving thou goest boldly against the Knower of thy secret. Thou hidest thyself from thy neighbor, but thou art in the sight of thy Watcher; thou concealest from thy slave, but no hidden thing is hidden from thy Ruler. Thinkest thou that thy state will profit thee when thy departure draweth near? or that thy wealth will deliver thee when thy deeds destroy thee? or that thy repentance will suffice for thee when thy foot slippeth? or that thy kindred will lean to thee in the day that thy judgment-place gathereth thee? How is it thou hast not walked in the highroad of guidance, and hastened the treatment of thy disease, and blunted the edge of thine iniquity, and restrained thyself---thy chief enemy? Is not death thy doom? What then is thy preparation? Is not gray hair thy warning? What then is thy excuse? And in the grave's niche thy sleeping-place? What dost thou say? And to God thy going? and who shall be thy defender? Oft hath the time awakened thee, but thou hast set thyself to slumber; and admonition hath drawn thee, but thou hast strained against it; and warnings have been manifest to thee, but thou hast made thyself blind; and truth hath been established to thee, but thou hast disputed it; and death hath bid thee remember, but thou hast sought to forget; and it hath been in thy power to impart of good, but thou hast not imparted. Thou preferrest money which thou mayest hoard before piety which thou mayest keep in mind: thou choosest a castle thou mayest rear rather than bounty thou mayest confer. Thou inclinest from the guide from whom thou mightest get guidance, to the pelf thou mayest gain as a gift; thou lettest the love of the raiment thou covetest overcome the recompense thou mightest earn. The rubies of gifts cling to thy heart more than the seasons of prayer; and the heightening of dowries is preferred with thee to continuance in almsgivings. The dishes of many meats are more desired to thee than the leaves of doctrines: the jesting of comrades is more cheerful to thee than the reading of the Qur'an. Thou commandest to righteousness, but violatest its sanctuary: thou forbiddest from deceit, but refrainest not thyself: thou turnest men from oppression, and then thou drawest near to it; thou fearest mankind, but God is more worthy that thou shouldest fear him. Then he recited:

Woe to him who seeks the world, and turna to it his careering: And recovers not from his greediness for it, and the excess of his love. Oh, if he were wise, but a drop of what he seeks would content him.

Then he laid his dust, and let his spittle subside; and put this bottle on his arm, and his staff under his armpit. And when the company gazed on his uprising, and saw that he equipped himself to move away from the midst, each of them put his hand into his bosom, and filled for him a bucket from his stream: and said, "Use this for thy spending, or divide it among thy friends." And he received it with half-closed eyes, and turned away from them, giving thanks; and began to take leave of whoever would escort him, that his road might be hidden from them; and to dismiss whoever would follow him, that his dwelling might be unknown. Said Al Harith, son of Hammam: Now I went after him, concealing from him my person; and followed on his track from where he could not see me; until he came to a cave, and slipped into it suddenly. So I waited for him 'till he put off his sandals and washed his feet, and then I ran in upon him; and found him sitting opposite an attendant, at some white bread and a roast kid, and over against them was a jar of date-wine. And I said to him, "Sirrah, was that thy story, and is this thy reality?" But he puffed the puff of heat and went near to burst with rage; and ceased not to stare at me >till I thought he would leap upon me. But when his fire was allayed, and his flame hid itself, he recited:

I don the black robe to seek my meal, and I fix my hook in the hardest prey: And of my preaching I make a noose, and steal with it against the chaser and the chased. Fortune has forced me to make way even to the lion of the thicket by the subtlety of my beguiling. Yet do I not fear its change, nor does my loin quiver at it: Nor does a covetous mind lead me to water at any well that will soil my honor. Now if Fortune were just in its decree it would not empower the worthless with authority.

Then he said to me, "Come and eat; or, if thou wilt, rise and tell." But I turned to his attendant, and said, "I conjure thee, by him through whom harm is deprecated, that thou tell me who is this." He said, "This is Abu Zayd, of Seruj, the light of foreigners, the crown of the learned." Then I turned back to whence I came, and was extreme in wonder at what I saw.

Al-Hariri Assemblies in Arab Literature

The Second Assembly

Al Harith, son of Hammam, related: Ever since my amulets were doffed and my turbans were donned, I was eager to visit learning's seat and to jade to it the camels of seeking, that through it I might cleave to what would be my ornament among men, my rain-cloud in thirst. And through the excess of my longing to kindle at it, and my desire to robe myself in its raiment, I discussed with every one, great and small, and sought my draught both of the rain-flood and the dew, and solaced myself with hope and desire. Now when I descended at Holwan, and had already tried the brethren, and tested their values, and proved what was worthless or fine, I found there Abu Zayd of Seruj, shifting among the varieties of pedigree, beating about in various courses of gain-getting; for at one time he claimed to be of the race of Sasan, and at another he made himself kin to the princes of Ghassan; and now he sallied forth in the vesture of poets; and anon he put on the pride of nobles. And yet with all this diversifying of his condition, and this display of contradiction, he is adorned with grace and information, and courtesy and knowledge, and astonishing eloquence, and obedient improvisation, and excelling accomplishments, and a foot that mounts the hills of the sciences. Now, through his goodly attainments he is associated with in spite of his faults; and through the largeness of his information there is a fondness for the sight of him; and through the blandishment of his fair-speaking men are loath to oppose him; and through the sweetness of his address he is helped to his desire. Then I clung to his skirts for the sake of his peculiar accomplishments, and valued highly his affection by reason of his precious qualities:

With him I wiped away my cares, and beheld my fortune displayed to me, open of face, gleaming with light. I looked upon his nearness to me as kinship, his abiding as wealth, his aspect as a full draught, his life as rain.

Thus we remained a long season; he produced for me daily some pleasantness, and drove some doubt from my heart, until the hand of want mixed for him the cup of parting, and the lack of a meal urged him to abandon Iraq; and the failures of supply cast him into desert regions, and the waving of the banner of distress ranged him in the line of travelers; and he sharpened for departure the edge of determination, and journeyed away, drawing my heart with his leading cord. *After he was gone none pleased me who kept by me, none filled me with affection by urging me to intimacy. Since he strayed away none has appeared to me his like in excellence; no friend has gotten the equal of his qualities.*

So he was hidden from me a season: I knew not his lair; I found none to tell of him; but when I had returned from my wandering to the place where my branch had sprouted, I was once present in the town library, which is the council-hall of scholars, the meeting-place of residents and strangers: Then there entered one with a thick beard and a squalid aspect, and he saluted those who sat, and took seat in the last rows of the people. Then began he to produce what was in his wallet, and to astonish those present by the sagacity of his judgment. And he said to the man who was next him, "What is the book into which thou lookest?" He said, "The poems of Abu 'Obadeh; him of whose excellence men bear witness." He said, "In what thou hast seen hast thou hit on any fine thing which thou admirest?" He said, "Yes; the line, *As though she smiled from strung pearls or hailstones, or camomile flowers.*

For it is original in the use of similitude which it contains." He said to him, "Here is a wonder! here is a lack of taste, Sir, thou hast taken for fat what is only swollen; thou hast blown on that which is no fuel: where art thou in comparison with the rare verse which unites the similitudes of the teeth?

My life a ransom for those teeth whose beauty charms, and which a purity adorns sufficing thee for all other. She parts her lips from fresh pearls, and from hail-stones, and from camomile-flowers, and from the palm-shoot, and from bubbles.

Then each one approved the couplet and admired it, and bade him repeat it and dictate it. And he was asked, "Whose is this verse, and is its author living or dead? He said, "By Allah, right is most worthy to be followed, and truth is most fitting to be listened to: Know, friends, that it is his who talks with you to-day." Said Al Harith: Now it was as though the company doubted of his fathering, and were unwilling to give credit to his claim. And he perceived what had fallen into their thoughts, and was aware of their inward unbelief; and was afraid that blame might chance to him, or ill-fame reach him; so he quoted from the Qur'an, "Some suspicions are a sin." Then he said, "O ye reciters of verse, physicians of sickly phrase!---Truly the purity of the gem is shown by the testing, and the hand of truth rends the cloak of doubt.---Now it was said aforetime that by trial is a man honored or contemned. So come! I now expose my hidden store to the proving, I offer my saddle-bag for comparison." Then hastened one who was there and said: "I know a verse such that there is no weaving on its beam, such that no genius can supply one after its image. Now, if thou wish to draw our hearts to thee, compose after this style:

She rained pearls from the daffodil, and watered the rose, and bit upon the 'unnab with hailstone.

And it was but the glance of an eye, or less, before he recited rarely:

I asked her when she met me to put off her crimson veil, and to endow my hearing with the sweetest of tidings: And she removed the ruddy light which covered the brightness of her moon, and she dropped pearls from a perfumed ring.

Then all present were astonished at his readiness, and acknowledged his honesty. And when he perceived that they approved his diction, and were hastening into the path of honoring him, he looked down the twinkling of an eye; then he said, "Here are two other verses for you"; and recited:

She came on the day when departure ardicted, in black robes, biting her fingers like one regretful, confounded: And night lowered on her morn, and a branch supported them both, and she bit into crystal with pearls.

Then did the company set high his value, and deem that his steady rain was a plenteous one; and they made pleasant their converse with him, and gave him goodly clothing. Said the teller of this story: Now when I saw the blazing of his firebrand, and the gleam of his unveiled brightness, I fixed a long look to guess at him, and made my eye to stray over his countenance. And lo! he was our Shaykh of Seruj; but now his dark night was moon-lit. Then I congratulated myself on his coming thither, and hastened to kiss his hand: and said to him, "What has changed thy appearance, so that I could not recognize thee? what has made thy beard gray, so that I knew not thy countenance?" And he indited and said:

The stroke of calamities makes us hoary, and fortune to men is a changer. If it yields today to any, tomorrow it overcomes him. Trust not the gleam of its lightning, for it is a deceitful gleam.

But be patient if it hounds calamities against thee, and drives them on. For there is no disgrace on the pure gold when it is turned about in the fire.

Then he rose and departed from his place, and carried away our hearts with him.

The Al-Hariri Assemblies in Arab Literature

Third Assembly

Al Harith, son of Hammam, related: I was set with some comrades in a company wherein he that made appeal was never bootless, and the rubbing of the fire-shafts never failed, and the flame of contention never blazed. And while we were catching from each other the cues of recitations, and betaking ourselves to novelties of anecdote, behold there stood by us one on whom was a worn garment, and in whose walk was a limp. And he said, O ye best of treasures, joys of your kindred: Health to you this morning; may ye enjoy your morning draught. took on one who was erewhile master of guest-room and largess, wealth and bounty, land and villages, dishes and feasting. But the frowning of calamities ceased not from him, and the warrings of sorrows, and the fire-flakes of the malice of the envious, and the succession of dark befallings, until the court was empty, and the yard was bare, and the fountain sank, and the dwelling was desolate, and the hall was void, and the chamber stone-strewed. And fortune shifted so that the household wailed; and the stalls were vacant, so that the rival had compassion; and the cattle and the goods they perished, so that the envious and malignant pitied. And to such a pass did we come, through assailing fortune and prostrating need, that we were shod with soreness, and fed on choking, and filled our bellies with ache, and wrapped our entrails upon hunger, and anointed our eyes with watching, and made pits our home, and deemed thorns a smooth bed, and came to forget our saddles, and thought destroying death to be sweet, and the ordained day to be tardy. And now is there any one generous to heal, bountiful to bestow? For by him who made me to spring from Kaylah, surely I am now a brother of penury, I have not a night's victual.

Said Al Harith, son of Hammam: Now I pitied his distresses, and inclined to the eliciting of his rhymes. So I drew forth for him a denar, and said to him, to prove him, "If thou praise it in verse it is thine, full surely." And he betook himself to recite on the spot, borrowing nothing:

How noble is that yellow one, whose yellowness is pure,
Which traverses the regions, and whose journeying is afar.
Told abroad are its fame and repute:
Its lines are set as the secret sign of wealth;
Its march is coupled with the success of endeavors;
Its bright look is loved by mankind;
As though its ore had been molten of their hearts.
By its aid whoever has gotten it in his purse assails boldly,
Though kindred be perished, or tardy to help.
Oh charming are its purity and brightness;
Charming are its sufficiency and help.
How many a ruler is there whose rule has been perfected by it!
How many a sumptuous one is there whose grief, but for it, would be endless!
How many a host of cares has one charge of it put to flight!
How many a full moon has a sum of it brought down!
How many a one burning with rage, whose coal is flaming,
Has it been secretly whispered to, and then his anger has softened.
How many a prisoner, whom his kin had

yielded,
Has it delivered, so that his gladness has been unmingled,
Now by the Truth of the Lord whose creation brought it forth,
Were it not for his fear, I should say its power is supreme.

Then he stretched forth his hand after his recitation, and said, "The honorable man performs what he promises, and the rain-cloud pours if it has thundered." So I threw him the dinar, and said, "Take it; no grudging goes with it." And he put it in his mouth and said, "God bless it." Then he girt up his skirts for departure, after that he had paid his thanks. But there arose in me, through his pleasantry, a giddiness of desire which made me ready to incur indebtedness. So I bared another dinar, and said, "Does it suit thee to blame this, and then gather it?" And he recited impromptu, and sang with speed:

Ruin on it for a deceiver and insincere,
The yellow one with two faces like a hypocrite!
It shows forth with two qualities to the eye of him that looks on it,
The adornment of the loved one, the color of the lover.

Affection for it, think they who judge truly,
Tempts men to commit that which shall anger their Maker.
But for it no thief's right hand were cut off;
Nor would tyranny be displayed by the impious
Nor would the niggard shrink from the night-farer;
Nor would the delayed claimant mourn the delay of him that withholds
Nor would men call to God from the envious who casts at them.
Moreover, the worst quality that it possesses
Is that it helps thee not in straits,
Save by fleeing from thee like a runaway slave.
Well done he who casts it away from a hill-top
And who, when it whispers to him with the whispering of a lover,
Says to it in the words of the truth-speaking, the veracious,
"I have no mind for intimacy with thee-begone!

Then said I to him, "How abundant is thy shower!" He said, "Agreement binds strongest." So I tossed him the second dinar and said, "Consecrate them both with the Twice-read Chapter." He cast it into his mouth and joined it with its twin, and turned away blessing his morning's walk, praising the assembly and its bounty. Said Al Harith, son of Hammam: Now my heart whispered me that he was Abu Zayd, and that his going lame was for a trick; so I called him back and said to him, "Thou art recognized by thy eloquence, so straighten thy walk." He said, "If thou be the son of Hammam, be thou greeted with honor and live long among the honorable." I said, "I am Harith; but what is thy condition amid all thy fortunes." He said, "I change between two conditions, distress and ease; and I veer with two winds, the tempest and the breeze." I said, "And how hast thou pretended lameness? the like of thee plays not buffoon." Then his cheerfulness, which had shone forth, waned; but he recited as he moved away:

I have feigned to be lame, not from love of lameness, but that I may knock at the gate of relief. For my cord is thrown on my neck, and I go as one who ranges freely. Now if men blame me I say, "Excuse me: sure there is no guilt on the lame."

Al-Hariri Assemblies in Arab Literature

The Fourth Assembly

Al Harith, son of Hammam, related: I journeyed to Damietta in a year of much coming and going, and in those days was I glanced after for my affluence, desired in friendship: I trained the bordered robes of wealth and looked upon the features of joy. And I was traveling with companions who had broken the staff of dissension, who were suckled on the milk-flows of concord, so that they showed like the teeth of a comb in uniformity, and like one soul in agreement of desires; but we coursed on withal apace, and not one of us but had saddled a fleet she-camel; and if we alighted at a station or went aside to a spring, we snatched the halt and lengthened not the staying.

Now it happened that we were urging our camels on a night youthful in prime, raven-locked of complexion; and we journeyed until the night-season had put off its prime, and the morning had wiped away the dye of the dark;

but when we wearied of the march and inclined to drowsiness, we came upon a ground with dew-moistened hillocks, and a faint east breeze: and we chose it as a resting-place for the white camels, an abode for the night-halt. Now when the caravan had descended there, and the groan and the roar of the beasts were still, I heard a loud-voiced man say to his talk-fellow in the camp, "What is the rule of thy conduct with thy people and neighbors?" The other answered, I am duteous to my neighbor though he wrong me; and give my fellowship even to the violent; and bear with a partner though he disorder my affairs; and love my friend even though he drench me with a tepid draught; and prefer my well-wisher above my brother; and fulfil to my comrade even though he requite me not with a tenth; and think little of much if it be of my guest; and whelm my companion with my kindness; and put my talk-fellow in the place of my prince; and hold my intimate to be as my chief; and commit my gifts to my acquaintance; and confer my comforts on my associate; and soften my speech to him that hates me; and continue to ask after him that disregards me; and am pleased with but the crumbs of my due; and am content with but the least portion of my reward; and complain not of wrong even when I am wronged; and revenge not, even though a viper sting me.

Then said his companion to him, Alas! my boy, only he who clings should be clung to; only he who is valuable should be prized. As for me I give only to him who will requite; I distinguish not the insolent by my regard; nor will I be of pure affection to one who refuses me fairdealing; nor treat as a brother one who would undo my tethering-rope; nor aid one who would baulk my hopes; nor care for one who would cut my cords; nor be courteous to him who ignores my value; nor give my leading rope to one who breaks my covenant; nor be free of my love to my adversaries; nor lay aside my menace to the hostile; nor plant my benefits on the land of my enemies; nor be willing to impart to him who rejoices at my ills; nor show my regard to him who will exult at my death; nor favor with my gifts any but my friends; nor call to the curing of my sickness any but those who love me; nor confer my friendship on him who will not stop my breach; nor make my purpose sincere to him who wishes my decease; nor be earnest in prayer for him who will not fill my wallet; nor pour out my praise on him who empties my jar. For who has adjudged that I should be lavish and thou shouldest hoard, that I should be soft and thou rough, that I should melt and thou freeze, that I should blaze and thou smolder? No, by Allah, but let us balance in speech as coin, and match in deed as sandals, that each to each we may be safe from fraud and free from hatred. For else, why should I give thee full water and thou stint me? why should I bear with thee and thou contemn me? why should I gain for thee and thou wound me? why should I advance to thee and thou repel me? For how should fair-dealing be attracted by injury? how can the sun rise clear with cloud? And when did love follow docilely after wrong? and what man of honor consents to a state of abasement? For excellently said thy father:

Whoso attaches his affection to me, I repay him as one who builds on his foundation:
And I mete to a friend as he metes to me, according to the fulness of his meting or its defect.
I make him not a loser! for the worst of men is he whose to-day falls short of his yesterday.
Whoever seeks fruit of me gets only the fruit of his own planting.
I seek not to defraud, but I will not come off with the bargain of one who is weak in his reason.
I hold not truth binding on me toward a man who holds it not binding on himself.

There may be some one insincere in love who fancies that I am true in my friendship for him, while he is false;
And knows not in his ignorance that I pay my creditor his debt after its kind. "Sunder, with the sundering of hate, from one who would make thee a fool, and hold him as one entombed in his grave.
And toward him in whose intercourse there is aught doubtful put on the garb of one who shrinks from his intimacy.
And hope not for affection from any who sees that thou art in want of his money.

Said Al Harith, son of Hammam: Now, when I had gathered what passed between them, I longed to know them in person. And when the sun shone forth, and robed the sky with light, I went forth before the camels had risen, and with an earliness beyond the earliness of the crow, and began to follow the direction of that night-voice, and to examine the faces with a searching glance: until I caught sight of Abu Zayd and his son talking together, and upon them were two worn mantles. Then I knew that they were my two talkers of the night, the authors of my recitation. So I approached them as one enamored of their refinement, pitying their shabbiness; and offered them a removal to my lodging, and the disposal of my much and my little; and began to tell abroad their worth among the travelers, and to shake for them the fruited branches; until they were overwhelmed with gifts, and taken as friends. Now we were in a night-camp, whence we could discern the build of the villages, and spy the fires of hospitality. And when Abu Zayd saw that his purse was full, and his distress removed, he said to me, "Truly my body is dirty, and my filth has caked: Wilt thou permit me to go to a village, and bathe, and fulfil this urgent need?" I said, "If thou wilt; but quick! return!" He said, "Thou shalt find me appear again to thee, quicker than the glancing of thine eye." Then he coursed away, as courses the good steed in the training-ground, and said to his son, "Haste! haste!" And we imagined not that he was deceiving, or seeking to escape. So we stayed and watched for him as men watch for the new moons of feasts, and made search for him by spies and scouts, until the sunlight was weak with age, and the wasted bank of the day had nigh crumbled in. Then, when the term of waiting had been prolonged, and the sun showed in faded garb, I said to my companions, "We have gone to the extreme in delay, and have been long in the setting forth; so that we have lost time, and it is plain that the man was lying. Now, therefore, prepare for the journey, and turn not aside to the greenness of dung-heaps." Then I rose to equip my camel and lade for the departure; and found that Abu Zayd had written on the pack-saddle:

Oh thou, who wast to me an arm and a helper, above all mankind! Reckon not that I have left thee through impatience or ingratitude: For since I was born I have been of those who "when they have eaten separate."

Said Al Harith: Then I made the company read the words of the Qur'an that were on the pack-saddle, so that he who had blamed him might excuse him. And they admired his witticism, but commanded themselves from his mischief. Then we set forth, nor could we learn whose company he had gotten in our place.

Al-Hariri Assemblies in Arab Literature

The Fifth Assembly

Al Harith, son of Hammam, related: I was conversing at Sufa, in a night whose complexion was of a two-fold hue, whose moon was as an amulet of silver, with companions who had been nourished on the milk of eloquence, who might draw the train of oblivion over Sahban. Each was a man to remember from, and not to guard against; each was one whom his friend would incline to, and not avoid. And the night talk fascinated us until the moon had set, and the watching overcame us. Now when night's unmingled dark had spread its awning, and there was naught but nodding among us, we heard from the gate the faint sound of a wayfarer, rousing the dogs; then followed the knock of one bidding to open. We said, "Who is it that comes in the dark night?" Then the traveler answered:

O people of the mansion, be ye guarded from ill!
Meet not harm as long as ye live!
Lo! the night which glooms has driven
To your abode one disheveled, dust-laden,
A brother of journeying, that has been lengthened, extended,
'Till he has become bent and yellow
Like the new moon of the horizon when it smiles.
And now he approaches your courtyard, begging boldly,
And repairs to you before all people else,
To seek from you food and a lodging.
Ye have in him a guest contented, ingenuous,
One pleased with all, whether sweet or bitter,
One who will withdraw from you, publishing your bounty.

Said Al Harith, son of Hammam: Now when we were caught by the sweetness of his utterance, and knew what was behind his lightning, we hastened to open the gate, and met him with welcome; and said to the boy "Quick, quick! bring what is ready!" Then said our guest, "Now, by him who has set me down at your abode, I will not roll my tongue over your food, unless ye pledge me that ye will not make me a burden, that ye will not, for my sake, task yourselves with a meal. For sometimes a morsel aches the eater, and forbids him his repasts. And the worst of guests is he who imposes trouble and annoys his host, and especially with a harm that affects the body and tends to sickness. For, by that proverb, which is widely current, >The best suppers are those that are clearly seen,' is only meant that supper-time should be hastened, and eating by night, which dims the sight, avoided. Unless, by Allah, the fire of hunger kindle and stand in the way of sleep." Said Al Harith: Now it was as though he had got sight of our desire, and so had shot with the bow of our conviction. Accordingly we gratified him by agreeing to the condition, and commended him for his easy temper. And when the boy brought what was to be had, and lighted the candle in the midst of us, I looked close at him, and lo! it was Abu Zayd. So I said to my company, "Joy to you of the guest who has come! Nay, but the spoil is lightly won! For if the moon of Sirius has gone down, truly the moon of poetry has risen: Or if the full moon of the Lion has waned, the full moon of eloquence shines forth." Then ran through them the wineglow of joy, and sleep few away from their eye-corners. And they refused the rest which they had purposed, and returned to the spreading out of pleasantry, after they had folded it. But Abu Zayd kept intent upon plying his hands; however, when what was before him might be removed, I said to him, "Present us with one of the rare stories from thy night talkings, or some wonder from among the wonders of thy journeys." He said, "Of wonders I have met with such as no seers have seen, no tellers have told. But among the most wondrous was that which I beheld tonight, a little before my visit to you and my coming to your gate." Then we bade him tell us of this new thing which he had seen in the field of his night-faring. He said, Truly the hurlings of exile have thrown me to this land: And I was in hunger and distress, with a scrip like the heart of the mother of Moses. Now, as soon as the dark had settled, I arose, in spite of all my footsoreness, to seek a host or to gain a loaf. Then the driver hunger, and Fate, which is by-named the Father of Wonders, urged me on, >till I stood at the door of a house, snd spoke, improvising:

Hail people of this dwelling,
May ye live in the ease of a plenteous life!
What have ye for a son of the road, one crushed to the sand,
Worn with journeys, stumbling in the night-dark night,
Aching in entrails, which enclose naught but

hunger?
For two days he has not tasted the savor of a meal:
In your land there is no refuge for him
And already the van of the drooping darkness has gloomed;
And through bewilderment he is in restlessness
Now in this abode is there any one, sweet of spring,
Who will say to me "Throw away thy staff and enter:
Rejoice in a cheerful welcome and a ready meal?"

Then came forth to me a lad in a tunic, and answered:

Now by the sanctity of the Shaykh who ordained hospitality,
And founded the House of Pilgrimage in the Mother of cities,
We have naught for the night-farer when he visits us
But conversation and a lodging in our hall
For how should he entertain whom hinders from sleepfulness
Hunger which peels his bones when it assails him?

Now what thinkest thou of my tales what thinkest thou?

I said, "What shall I do with an empty house, and a host the ally of penury? But tell me, youth, what is thy name, for thy understanding has charmed me." He said, "My name is Zayd, and my birth-place Fayd: and I came to this city yesterday with my mother's kindred of the Benu 'Abs.=" I said to him, "Show me further, so mayest thou live and be raised when thou fallest!" He said, "My mother Barrah told me (and she is like her name, >pious') that she married in the year of the foray on Mawan a man of the nobles of Seruj and Ghassan; but when he was aware of her pregnancy (for he was a crafty bird, it is said) he made off from her by stealth, and away he has stayed, nor is it known whether he is alive and to be looked for, or whether he has been laid in the lonely tomb." Said Abu Zayd, "Now I knew by sure signs that he was my child; but the emptiness of my hand turned me from making known to him, so I parted from him with heart crushed and tears unsealed. And now, ye men of understanding, have ye heard aught more wondrous than this wonder?" We said, "No, by him who has knowledge of the Book." He said, "Record it among the wonders of chance; bid it abide forever in the hearts of scrolls; for nothing like it has been told abroad in the world." Then he bade bring the ink flask, and its snake-like reeds, and we wrote the story elegantly as he worded it; after which we sought to draw from him his wish about receiving his boy. He said, "If my purse were heavy, then to take charge of my son would be light." We said, "If a *nisab* of money would suffice thee, we will collect it for thee at once." He said, "And how should a nisab not content me? would any but a madman despise such a sum?" Said the narrator, Then each of us undertook a share of it, and wrote for him an order for it. Whereupon he gave thanks for the kindness, and exhausted the plenteousness of praise; until we thought his speech long, or our merit little. And then he spread out such a bright mantle of talk as might shame the stuffs of Yemen, until the dawn appeared and the light-bearing morn went forth. So we spent a night of which the mixed hues had departed, until its hind-locks grew gray in the dawn; and whose lucky stars were sovereign until its branch budded into light. But when the limb of the sun peeped forth, he leaped up as leaps the gazelle, and said, "Rise up, that we may take hold on the gifts and draw payment of the checks: for the clefts of my heart are widening through yearning after my child." So I went with him, hand in hand, to make easy his success. But as soon as he had secured the coin in his purse the marks of his joy flashed forth, and he said, "Be thou rewarded for the steps of thy feet! be God my substitute toward thee!" I said, "I wish to follow thee that I may behold thy noble child, and speak with him that he may answer eloquently." Then looked he at me as looks the deceiver on the deceived, and laughed >till his eyeballs gushed with tears; and he recited:

O thou who didst fancy the mirage to be water when I quoted to thee what I quoted! I thought not that my guile would be hidden, or that it would be doubtful what I meant. By Allah, I have no Barrah for a spouse; I have no son from whom to take a by-name. Nothing is mine but divers kinds of magic, in which I am original and copy no one: They are such as Al Asma'i tells not of in what he has told; such as Al Komayt never wove. These I use when I will to reach whatever my hand would pluck: And were I to abandon them, changed would be my state, nor should I gain what I now gain. So allow my excuse; nay, pardon me, if I have done wrong or crime.

Then he took leave of me and passed away, and set coals of the *ghada* in my breast.

Al-Hariri Assemblies in Arab Literature

The Sixth Assembly

Al Harith, son of Hammam, related: I was present in the Court of Supervision at Meraghah when the talk ran of eloquence. Then agreed all who were there of the knights of the pen, and the lords of genius, that there remained no one who could select his diction, or use himself freely in it as he willed: and that since the men of old were gone, there was none now left who could originate a brilliant method, or open a virgin style. And that even one marvelous among the writers of this age, and holding in his grasp the cords of eloquence, is but a dependent on the ancients, even though he possess the fluency of

Sahban Wa'il. Now there was in the assembly an elderly man, sitting on the outskirts, in the places of the attendants: and as often as the company overran in their career, and scattered fruit, good and bad, from their store, the side-glance of his eye and the up-turning of his nose showed that he was one silent to spring, one crouching who would extend his stride: that he was a twanger of the bow who shapes his arrows, one who sits in wait desiring the conflict. But when the quivers were empty, and quiet returned; when the storms had fallen, and the disputer was stayed, he turned to the company and said, Ye have uttered a grievous thing; ye have wandered much from the way: for ye have magnified moldering bones; ye have been excessive in your leaning to those who are gone; ye have contemned your generation, among whom ye were born, and with whom your friendships are established. Have ye forgotten, ye skilful in testing, ye sages of loosing and binding, how much new springs have given forth; how the colt has surpassed the full-grown steed; in refined expressions, and delightful metaphors, and ornate addresses, and admired cadences? And, if any one here will look diligently, is there in the ancients aught but ideas whose paths are worn, whose ranges are restricted; which have been handed down from them through the priority of their birth, not from any superiority in him who draws first at the well over him who comes after? Now truly know I one who, when he composes, colors richly; and when he expresses, embellishes; and when he is lengthy, finds golden thoughts; and when he is brief, baffles his imitator; and when he improvises, astonishes; and when he creates, cuts the envious.

Then said to him the President of the Court, the Eye of those Eyes: "Who is it that strikes on this rock, that is the hero of these qualities?" He said, "It is the adversary of this thy skirmish, the partner of thy disputation: Now, if thou wilt, rein a good steed, call forth one who will answer, so shalt thou see a wonder." He said to him, "Stranger, the chough in our land is not taken for an eagle, and with us it is easy to discern between silver and shingle. Rare is he who exposes himself to the conflict, and then escapes the mortal hurt; or who stirs up the dust of trial, and then catches not the mote of contempt. So offer not thy honor to shame, turn not from the counsel of the counselor." He answered, "Each man knows best the mark of his arrow, and be sure the night shall disclose its morn."

Then whispered the company as to how his well should be fathomed, and his proving undertaken. Said one of them, "Leave him to my share, that I may pelt him with the stone of my story; for it is the tightest of knots, the touchstone of testing." Then they invested him with the command in this business as the Rebels invested Abu Na'ameh. Whereupon he turned to the elder and said, Know that I am attached to this Governor and maintain my condition by ornamental eloquence. Now, in my country, I could rely for the straightening of my crookedness on the sufficiency of my means, coupled with the smallness of my family. But when my back was weighted, and my thin rain failed, I repaired to him from my home with hope, and besought him to restore my comeliness and my competence. And he looked pleasantly on my coming, and was gracious, and served me morn and even. But when I sought permission from him to depart to my abode, on the shoulder of cheerfulness, he said, "I have determined that I will not provide thee with supplies, I will bring together for thee no scattered means, unless, before thy departure, thou compose an address, setting in it an exposition of thy state; such, that the letters of one of every two words shall all have dots, while the letters of the other shall not be pointed at all." And now have I waited for my eloquence a twelvemonth, but it has returned me not a word; and I have roused my wit for a year, but only my sluggishness has increased. And I have sought aid among the gathering of the scribes, but each of them has frowned and drawn back. Now, if thou hast disclosed thy character with accuracy, *Come with a Sign, if thou be of the truthful.*

Then answered the elder, "Thou hast put a good steed to the pace; thou hast sought water at a full stream; thou hast given the bow to him who fashioned it; thou hast lodged in the house him who built it." And he thought a while >till he had let his flow of wit collect, his milch-camel fill her udder: and then he said: Wool thy ink-flask, and take thy implements and write: "Generosity (may God establish the host of thy successes) adorns; but meanness (may fortune cast down the eyelid of thy enviers) dishonors; the noble rewards, but the base disappoints; the princely entertains, but the niggard frights away; the liberal nourishes, but the churl pains; giving relieves, but deferring torments; blessing protects, and praise purifies; the honorable repays, for repudiation abases; the rejection of him who should be respected is error; a denial to the sons of hope is outrage; and none is miserly but the fool, and none is foolish but the miser;

and none hoards but the wretched; for the pious clenches not his palms.

"But thy promise ceases not to fulfil; thy sentiments cease not to relieve; nor thy clemency to indulge; nor thy new moon to illumine; nor thy bounty to enrich; nor thy enemies to praise thee; nor thy blade to destroy; nor thy princeship to buildup; nor thy suitor to gain; nor thy praiser to win; nor thy kindness to succor; nor thy heaven to rain; nor thy milk-flow to abound; nor thy refusal to be rare. Now he who hopes in thee is an old man like a shadow, one to whom nothing remains. He seeks thee with a persuasion whose eagerness leaps onward; he praises thee in choice phrases, which merit their dowries. His demand is a light one, his claims are clear; his praise is striven for, his blame is shunned. And behind him is a household whom misery has touched, whom wrong has stripped, whom squalor involves. And he is ever in tears that come at call, and trouble that melts him, and care that is as a guest, and growing sadness: on account of hope that has disappointed him, and loss that has made him hoary, and the enemy that has fixed tooth in him, and the quiet that is gone. And yet his love has not swerved, that there should be anger at him; nor is his wood rotten, that he should be lopped away; nor has his breast spit foulness that he should be shaken off; nor has his intercourse been froward that he should be hated. Now thy honor admits not the rejection of his claim, so whiten his hope by the lightening of his distress: then will he publish thy praise throughout the world. So mayest thou live to avert misfortune, and to bestow wealth; to heal grief and to care for the aged: attended by affluence and fresh joyousness; as long as the hall of the rich is visited, or the delusion of the selfish is feared. And so Peace."

Now when he had ceased from the dictation of his address, and showed forth his prowess in the strife of eloquence, the company gratified him both by word and deed, and made large to him their courtesy and their bounty. Then was he asked from what tribe was his origin, and in what valley was his lair; and he answered:

Ghassan is my noble kindred, and Seruj my ancient land:
There my home was like the sun in splendor and mighty rank
And my dwelling was as paradise in sweetness and pleasantness and worth.
Oh, excellent were the life I led there and the plenteous delights,

In the day that I drew my broidered robe in its meadow, sharp of purpose,
I walked proudly in the mantle of youth and looked upon goodly pleasures
Fearing not the visitations of time and its evil haps.
Now if grief could kill, surely I should perish from my abiding griefs;
Or if past life could be redeemed my good heart's blood should redeem it.
For death is better for a man than to live the life of a beast.
When the ring of subjection leads him to mighty trouble and outrage,
And he sees lions whom the paws of assailing hyenas seize.
But the fault is in the time: but for its ill luck character would not miss its place:
If the time were upright, then would the conditions of men be upright in it.

After this his story reached the Governor, who filled his mouth with pearls, and bade him join himself to his followers, and preside over his court of public writing. But the gifts sufficed him, and unwillingness restrained him from office. Said the narrator: Now I had recognized the wood of his tree before the ripening of his fruit: And I had nigh roused the people to the loftiness of his worth before that his full moon shone forth. But he hinted to me by a twinkle of his eyelid that I should not bare his sword from its sheath. And when he was going forth, full of purse, and parting from us, having gotten victory, I escorted him, performing the duty of respect, and chiding him for his refusal of office. But he turned away with a smile and recited with a chant:

Sure to traverse the lands in poverty is dearer to me than rank:
For in rulers there is caprice and fault-finding, oh what faultfinding!
There is none of them who completes his good work,
Or who builds up where has laid foundation.
So let not the glare of the mirage beguile thee;
Undertake not that which is doubtful:
For how many a dreamer has his dream made joyful;
But fear has come upon him when he waked.

Al-Hariri Assemblies in Arab Literature

The Seventh Assembly

Al Harith, son of Hammam, related: I had determined on journeying from Barka'id; but now I noted the signs of the coming feast, and I disliked to set forth from the city until I had witnessed there the day of adornment. So when it came on with its rites, bounden or of free will, and brought up its horsemen and footmen, I followed the tradition in new apparel, and went forth with the people to keep festival. Now when the congregation of the prayer-court was gathered and ranged, and the crowding took men's breath, there appeared an old man in a pair of cloaks, and his eyes were closed: and he bore on his arm what was like a horse-bag, and had for a guide an old woman like a goblin. Then he stopped, as stops one tottering to sink, and greeted with the greeting of him whose voice is feeble. And when he had made an end of his salutation he circled his five fingers in his wallet, and brought forth scraps of paper that had been written on with colors of dyes in the season of leisure, and gave them to his old beldame, bidding her to detect each simple one. So whenever she perceived of any that his hand was moist in bounty, she cast one of the papers before him. Said Al Harith: Now cursed fate allotted to me a scrap whereon was written:

Sure I have become crushed with pains and fears;
Tried by the proud one, the crafty, the assailer
By the traitor among my brethren, who hates me for my need,
By jading from those who work to undo my toils.
How oft do I burn through spites and penury and wandering;
How oft do I tramp in shabby garb, thought of

by none.
Oh, would that fortune when it wronged me had slain my babes!
For were not my cubs torments to me and ills,
I would not have addressed my hopes to kin or lord:
Nor would I draw my skirts along the track of abasement.
For my garret would be more seemly for me, and my rags more honorable.
Now is there a generous man who will see that the lightening of my loads must be by a denar;
Or will quench the heat of my anxiety by a shirt and trousers?

Said Al Harith, son of Hammam: Now when I had looked on the garb of the verses, I longed for a knowledge of him who wove it, the broiderer of its pattern. And my thought whispered to me that the way to him was through the old woman, and advised me that a fee to an informer is lawful. So I watched her, and she was wending through the rows, row by row, begging a dole of the hands, hand by hand. But not at all did the trouble prosper her; no purse shed aught upon her palm. Wherefore when her soliciting was baffled, and her circuit wearied her, she commended herself to God with the "Return," and addressed herself to collect the scraps of paper. But the devil made her forget the scrap that I held, and she turned not aside to my spot: but went back to the old man weeping at the denial, complaining of the oppression of the time. And he said, "In God's hands I am, to God I commit my case; there is no strength or power but by God," then he recited:

There remains not any pure, not any sincere; not a spring, not a helper: But of baseness there is one level; not any is trusty, not any of worth.

Then said he to her, "Cheer thy soul and promise it good; collect the papers and count them." She said, "Truly I counted them when I asked them back, and I found that one of them the hand of loss had seized." He said, "Perdition on thee, wretch; shall we be hindered, alas, both of the prey and the net, both of the brand and the wick? surely this is a new handful to the load." Then did the old woman hasten back, retracing her path to seek her scroll; and when she drew near to me I put with the paper a dirhem and a mite, and said to her, "If thou hast a fondness for the polished, the engraved (and I pointed to the dirhem), show me the secret, the obscure; but if thou willest not to explain, take then the mite and begone." Then she inclined to the getting of that whole full moon, the bright-faced, the large. So she said, "Quit contention and ask what thou wilt." Whereupon I asked her of the old man and his country, of the poem, and of him who wove its mantle. She said, "Truly, the old man is of the people of Seruj, and he it was who broidered that woven poem." Then she snatched the dirhem with the snatch of a hawk, and shot away as shoots the darting arrow. But it troubled my heart that perchance it was Abu Zayd who was indicated, and my grief kindled at his mishap with his eyes. And I should have preferred to have gone suddenly on him and talked to him, that I might test the quality of my discernment upon him. But I was unable to come to him save by treading on the necks of the congregation, a thing forbidden in the law; and, moreover, I was unwilling that people should be annoyed by me, or that blame should arrive to me. So I cleaved to my place, but made his form the fetter of my sight, until the sermon was ended, and to leap to him was lawful. Then I went briskly to him and examined him in spite of the closing of his eyelids. And, lo! my shrewdness was as the shrewdness of Ibn 'Abbas, and my discernment as the discernment of Iyas. So at once I made myself known, and presented him with one of my tunics, and bade him to my bread. And he was joyful at my bounty and recognition, and acceded to the call to my loaves; and he set forth, and my hand was his leading cord, my shadow his conductor; and the old woman was the third prop of the pot; yes, by the Watcher from whom no secret is hidden! Now, when he had taken seat in my nest, and I had set before him what hasty meal was in my power, he said, "Harith, is there with us a third?" I said, "There is none but the old woman." He said, "From her no secret is withheld." Then he opened his eyes and stared round with the twin balls, and, lo! the two lights of his face kindled like the Farkadan. And I was joyful at the safety of his sight, but marveled at the strangeness of his ways. Nor did quiet possess me, nor did patience fit with me, until I asked him, "What led thee to feign blindness; thou, with thy journeying in desolate places, and thy traversing of wildernesses, and thy pushing into far lands." But he made show as if his mouth were full, and kept as though busied with his meal, until, when he had fulfilled his need, he sharpened his look upon me and recited:

Since Time (and he is the father of mankind) makes himself blind to the right in his purposes and aims, I too have assumed blindness, so as to be called a brother of it. What wonder that one should match himself with his father!

Then said he to me, "Rise, and go to the closet, and fetch me alkali that may clear the eye, and clean the hand, and soften the skin, and perfume the breath, and brace the gums, and strengthen the stomach: and let it be clean of box, fragrant of odor, new of pounding, delicate of powdering; so that one touching it shall count it to be eye-paint, and one smelling it shall fancy it to be camphor. And join with it a toothpick choice in material, delightful in use, goodly in shape, that invites to the repast: and let it have the slimness of a lover, and the polish of a sword, and the sharpness of the lance of war, and the pliancy of a green bough." Said Al Harith: Then I rose to do what he bade that I might rid him of the trace of his food; and thought not that he purposed to deceive by sending me into the closet; nor suspected that he was mocking of his messenger when he called for the alkali and toothpick. But when I returned with what was asked for, in less than the drawing of a breath, I found that the hall was empty, and that the old man and woman had sped away. Then was I extreme in anger at his deceit, and I pressed on his track in search of him; but he was as one who is sunk in the sea, or has been borne aloft to the clouds of heaven.

Al-Hariri Assemblies in Arab Literature

The Eighth Assembly

Al Harith, son of Hammam, related: Among the wonders of time, I saw that two suitors came before the Qadi of Ma'arrat an No'man. From the one of them the two excellencies of life had departed, while the other was as a bough of the ben tree. And the old man said: God strengthen the judge, as by him he strengthens whoever seeks judgment. Behold I had a slave girl, elegant of shape, smooth of cheek, patient to labor; at one time she ambled like a good steed, at another she slept quietly in her bed: even in July thou wouldst feel her touch to be cool. She had understanding and discretion, sharpness and wit, a hand with fingers, but a mouth without teeth: yet did she pique as with tongue of snake, and saunter in training robe; and she was displayed in blackness and whiteness; and she drank, but not from cisterns. She was now truth-telling, now beguiling; now hiding, now peeping forth; yet fitted for employment, obedient in poverty and in wealth: if thou didst spurn she showed affection, but if thou didst put her from thee, she remained quietly apart. Generally would she serve thee, and be courteous to thee, though sometimes she might be froward to thee and pain thee, and trouble thee. Now this youth asked her service of me for a purpose of his own, and I made her his servant, without reward, on the condition that he should enjoy the use of her, but not burden her with more than she could bear. But he forced on her too hard a work, and exacted of her long labor; then returned her to me broken in health, offering a compensation which I accept not.

Then said the youth: Sure the old man is more truthful than the Kata: but as for my hurting her it fell out by mistake. And now have I pledged to him in payment of his damage, a slave of mine, of equal birth as regards either kin, tracing his lineage to Al Kayn, free from stain and disgrace, whose place was the apple of his master's eye. He showed forth kindness, and called up admiration; he nourished mankind, and set guard on his tongue. If he was placed in power he was generous, if he marked aught for his own he was noble with it; if he was supplied he gave of his supply, and when he was asked for more he added. He stayed not in the house, and rarely visited his wives, save two by two. He was generous with his possession, he was lofty in his bounty; he kept with his spouse although she was not of his own clay; and there was pleasure in his comeliness, although he was not desired for his effeminacy.

Then said to them the Qadi, "Now either explain or depart." Then pressed forward the lad, and said:

He lent me a needle to darn my rags, which use has worn and blackened;
And its eye broke in my hand by chance, as I drew the thread through it.
But the old man would not forgive me the paying for it when he saw that it was spoiled;
But said, "Give me a needle like it, or a price, after thou hast mended it."
And he keeps my kohl-pencil by him as a pledge: oh, the shame that he has gotten by so doing:
For my eye is dry through giving him this pledge; my hand fails to ransom its anointer.

Now by this statement fathom the depth of my misery and pity one unused to bear it.

Then turned the Qadi to the old man, and said, "Come, speak without glozing," and he said:

*I swear by the holy place of sacrifice, and the devout whom the slope of Mina brings together
If the time had been my helper, thou wouldst not have seen me taking in pledge
The pencil which he has pledged to me.
Nor would I bring myself to seek a substitute for a needle that he had spoiled;
No, nor the price of it.
But the bow of calamities shoots at me with deadly arrows from here and there:
And to know my condition is to know his, misery, and distress and exile, and sickness.
Fortune has put us on a level: I am his like in misery, and he is as I.
He can not ransom his pencil now that it lies pledged in my hand:
And, through the narrowness of my own means, It is not within my bounds to forgive him for his offending.
Now this is my tale and his: so look upon us, And judge between us, and pity us.*

Now when the Qadi had learned their stories, and was aware of their penury and their distinction, he took out for them a denar from under his prayer-cushion, and said, "With this end and decide your contention." But the old man caught it before the youth, and claimed the whole of it in earnest, not in jest, saying to the youth, "Half is mine as my share of the bounty, and thy share is mine, in payment for my needle: nor do I swerve from justice, so come and take thy pencil." Now there fell on the youth, at the words of the old man, a sadness at which the heart of the Qadi grew sullen, stirring its sorrow for the lost dinar. Yet did he cheer the concern of the youth and his anguish by a few dirhems which he doled to him. Then he said to the two, "Avoid transactions, and put away disputes, and come not before me with wranglings, for I have no purse of fine-money for you." And they rose to go out from him, rejoicing at his gift, fluent in his praise. But as for the Qadi, his ill-humor subsided not after his stone had dripped; his sad look cleared not away after his rock had oozed. But when he recovered from his fit he turned to his attendants, and said, "Thy perception is imbued with the thought, and my guess announces to me, that these are practisers of craft, not suitors in a claim: but what is the way to fathom them, and to draw forth their secret?"

Then said to him the Knowing One of his assemblage, the Light of his following: "Surely the discovery of what they hide must be through themselves." So he bade an attendant follow them and bring them back; and when they stood before him he said to them, "Tell me truly your camel's age: so shall ye be secure from the consequence of your deceit." Then did the lad shrink back and ask for pardon; but the old man stepped forward and said:

I am the Seruji and this is my son; and the cub at the proving is like the lion.
Now never has his hand nor mine done wrong in matter of needle or pencil:
But only fortune, the harming, the hostile, has brought us to this, that we came forth to beg
Of each one whose palm is moist, whose spring is sweet;
Of each whose palm is close, whose hand is fettered;
By every art, and with every aim: by earnest, if it prosper, and if not, by jest.
That we may draw forth a drop for our thirsty lot, and consume our life in wretched victual.
And afterward Death is on the watch for us: if he fall not on us today he will fall tomorrow.

Then said the Qadi to him, "Oh rare! how admirable are the breathings of thy mouth; well done! should I say of thee, were it not for the guile that is in thee. Now know that I am of those that warn thee, and will beware of thee. So act not again deceitfully with judges, but fear the might of those who bear rule. For not every minister will excuse, and not at every season will speech be listened to." Then the old man promised to follow his counsel, and to abstain from disguising his character. And he departed from the Qadi's presence, while the guile beamed from his forehead. Said Al Harith, son of Hammam: Now I never saw aught more wonderful than these things in the changes of my journeys, nor read aught like them in the records of books.

Al-Hariri Assemblies in Arab Literature

The Ninth Assembly

Al Harith, son of Hammam, related: The liveliness of youth and the desire of gain sped me on until I had traversed all that is between Farghanah and Ghanah. And I dived into depths to gather fruits, and plunged into perils to reach my needs. Now I had caught from the lips of the learned, and understood from the commandments of the wise, that it behooves the well-bred, the sagacious, when he enters a strange city, to conciliate its Qadi and possess himself of his favor: that his back may be strengthened in litigation, that he may be secure in a strange land from the wrong of the powerful. So I took this doctrine as my guide and made it the leading-cord to my advantages. And I entered not a city, I went not into a lair, but I mingled myself with its judge as water is mingled with wine, and strengthened myself by his patronage as bodies are strengthened by souls. Now while I was in presence of the judge of Alexandria one cold evening, and he had brought out the alms-money to divide it among the needy, behold there entered an ill-looking old man whom a young matron dragged along. And she said: God strengthen the Qadi and through him make concord to be lasting: know that I am a woman of stock the most noble, of root the most pure, of mother's and father's kin the most honorable: my character is moderation, my disposition is contentment; my nature is to be a goodly help-meet; between me and my neighlsors is a wide difference. Now whenever there wooed me any who had built up honor or were lords of wealth my father silenced and chid them and mis liked their suit and their gift: making plea that he had covenanted with God Most High that he would not ally himself save with the master of a handicraft. Then did Providence destine for my calamity and pain that this deceiver should present himself in my father's hall; and swear among his people that he fulfilled his condition: asserting that long time he had strung pearl to pearl and sold them for great price. Then was my father deceived by the gilding of his falsehood, and married me to him before proving his condition. And when he had drawn me forth from my covert, and carried me away from my people, and removed me to his habitation, and brought me under his bond, I found him slothful, a sluggard; I discovered him to be a lie-a-bed, a slumberer. Now I had come to him with apparel and goodly show, with furniture and affluence. But he ceased not to sell it in a losing market and to squander the price in greedy feeding, until he had altogether destroyed whatever was mine, and spent my property on his need. So when he had made to me to forget the taste of rest and left my house cleaner than my hand's palm, I said to him, "Sir, know that there is no concealment after distress, no perfume after the wedding. Rise up then to gain something by thy trade, to gather the fruit of thy skill." But he declared that his trade had been struck with slackness through the violence that was abroad in the earth. Also I have a boy by him, thin as a toothpick: neither of us gets a fill by him, and through hunger our weeping to him ceases not. So I have brought him to thee and set him before thee, that thou mayest test the substance of his assertion, and decide between us as God shall show thee.

Then turned the Qadi to him and said: "Thou hast heard thy wife's story; now testify of thyself: else will I discover thy deceit and bid thy imprisonment." But he looked down as looks the serpent; then girt up his garment for a long strife, and said:

Hear my story, for it is a wonder; there is laughter in its tale, and there is wailing.
I am a man on whose qualities there is no blame, neither is there suspicion on his glory.
Seruj is my home where I was born, and my stock is Ghassan when I trace my lineage
And study is my business; to dive deep in learning is my pursuit;
And, oh! how excellent a seeking.
And my capital is the magic of speech, out of which are molded both verse and prose.
I dive into the deep of eloquence, and from it I choose the pearls and select them
I cull of speech the ripe fruit and the new; while another gathers but firing of the wood
I take the phrase of silver and when I have molded it men say that it is gold.
Now formerly I drew forth wealth by the learning I had gotten; I milked by it
And my foot's sole in its dignity mounted to ranges above which were no higher steps.
Oft were the presents brought in pomp to my dwelling, but I accepted not every one who gave.
But today learning is the chattel of slackest sale in the market of him on whom hope depends.

The honor of its sons is not respected; neither are relationship and alliance with them regarded.
It is as though they were corpses in their courtyards,
From whose stench men withdraw and turn aside.
Now my heart is confounded through my trial by the times; strange is their changing.
The stretch of my arm is straitened through the straitness of my hand's means;
Cares and grief assail me.
And my fortune, the blameworthy, has led me to the paths of that which honor deems base.
For I sold until there remained to me not a mat nor household goods to which I might turn.
So I indebted myself until I had burdened my neck by the carrying
Of a debt such that ruin had been lighter.
Then five days I wrapped my entrails upon hunger; but when the hunger scorched me,
I could see no goods except her outfit, in the selling of which I might go about and bestir myself.
So I went about with it; but my soul was loathing, and my eye tearful, and my heart saddened.
But when I made free with it, I passed not the bound of her consent,

That her wrath should rise against me.
And if what angers her be her fancying that it was my fingers that should make gain by stringing;
Or that when I purposed to woo her I tinseled my speech that my need might prosper:
I swear by him to whose Ra'beh the companies journey when the fleet camels speed them onward,
That deceit toward chaste ladies is not of my nature, nor are glozing and lying my badge.
Since I was reared naught has attached to my hand save the swiftly moving reeds and the books:
For it is my wit that strings necklaces, not my hand; what is strung is my poetry, and not chaplets.
And this is the craft I meant as that by which I gathered and gained.
So give ear to my explaining, as thou hast given ear to her;
And show respect to neither, but judge as is due.

Now when he had completed the structure of his story and perfected his recitation, the Qadi turned to the young woman, being heart-struck at the verses, and said, Know that it is settled among all judges and those who bear authority that the race of the generous is perished, and that the times incline to the niggardly. Now I imagine that thy husband is truthful in his speech, free from blame. For lo! he has acknowledged the debt to thee, and spoken the clear truth; he has given proof that he can string verses, and it is plain that he is bared to the bone. Now to vex him who shows excuse is baseness, to imprison the destitute is a sin: to conceal poverty is self-denial, to await relief with patience is devotion. So return to thy chamber and pardon the master of thy virginity: refrain from thy sharpness of tongue and submit to the will of thy Lord. Then in the almsgiving he assigned them a portion, and of the dirhems he gave them a pinch; and said to them, "Beguile yourselves with this drop, moisten yourselves with this driblet: and endure against the fraud and the trouble of the time, for it may be that God will bring victory or some ordinance from himself.=" Then they arose to go, and on the old man was the joy of one loosed from the bond, and the exulting of one who is in affluence after need.

Said the narrator: Now I knew that he was Abu Zayd in the hour that his sun peeped forth and his spouse reviled him: and I went near to declare his versatility and the fruiting of his divers branches. But then I was afraid that the

Qadi would hit on his falsehood and the lacking of his tongue, and not see fit, when he knew him, to train him to his bounty. So I forebore from speech with the forbearing of one who doubts, and I folded up mention of him as the roll is folded over the writing: save that when he had departed and had come whither he was to come, I said, "If there were one who would set out on his track, he might bring us the kernel of his story, and what tissues he is spreading forth." Then the Qadi sent one of his trusty ones after him and bade him to spy out of his tidings. But he delayed not to return bounding in, and to come back loudly laughing. Said the Qadi to him, "Well, Abu Maryam!" He said, "I have seen a wonder; I have heard what gives me a thrill." Said the Qadi to him, "What hast thou seen, and what is it thou hast learned?" He said, "Since the old man went forth he has not ceased to clap with his hands and to caper with his feet and to sing with the full of his cheeks: *I was near falling into trouble through an impudent jade; And should have gone to prison but for the Qadi of Alexandria.*

Then the Qadi laughed 'till his hat fell off, and his composure was lost: but when he returned to gravity and had followed excess by prayer for pardon, he said, "O God, by the sanctity of thy most honored servants, forbid that I should imprison men of letters." Then said he to that trusty one, "Hither with him!" and he set forth earnest in the search; but returned after a while, telling that the man was gone. Then said the Qadi, "Know that if he had been here he should have had no cause to fear, for I would have imparted to him as he deserves; I would have shown him that the latter state is better for him than the former." Said Al Harith, son of Hammam, Now, when I saw the leaning of the Qadi toward him, and that yet the fruit of the Qadi's notice was lost to him, there came on me the repentance of Al Farazdak when he put away Nawar, or of Al Sosa'i when the daylight appeared.

Al-Hariri Assemblies in Arab Literature

The Tenth Assembly

Al Harith, son of Hammam, related: The summoning of desire called me to Rahbah, the city of Malik, son of Towk, and I obeyed it, mounted on a fleet camel, and unsheathing an active purpose. Now when I had cast my anchors there, and fastened my ropes, and had gone forth from the bath after shaving my head, I saw a boy cast in the mold of comeliness, and clothed by beauty in the garb of perfection; and an old man was holding on to his sleeve, asserting that he had slain his son; but the boy denied knowledge of him and was horror-struck at his suspicion; and the contention between them scattered its sparks, and the crowding upon them was made up of good and bad. Now after their quarreling had been excessive, they agreed to refer to the Governor of the town; so they hastened to his court with the speed of Sulayk in his career; and when they were there the old man renewed his charge and claimed help. So the Governor made the boy speak, for the boy had already fascinated him by the graces of his bright brow, and cloven his understanding by the disposition of his forelocks. And the boy said, "It is the lie of a great liar against one who is no blood-shedder, and the slander of a knave against one who is not an assassin." Then said the Governor to the old man, "If two just Muslims testify for thee, well; if not, demand of him the oath." Said the old man, "Surely he struck him down remote from men, and shed his blood when alone; and how can I have a witness, when on the spot there was no beholder? But empower me to dictate an oath that it may appear to thee whether he speaks true or lies." He said to him, "Thou hast authority for that; thou with thy vehement grief for thy slain son." Then said the old man to the boy: Say, I swear by him who hath adorned foreheads with forelocks, and eyes with their black and white, and eyebrows with separation, and smiling teeth with regularity, and eyelids with languor, and noses with straightness, and cheeks with flame, and mouths with purity, and fingers with softness, and waists with slenderness, that I have not killed thy son by negligence, nor of wilfulness, nor made his head a sheath to my sword; if it be otherwise, may God strike my eyelid with soreness, and my cheek with freckles, and my forelocks with dropping, and my palm-shoot with greenness, and my rose with the ox-eye and my musk with a foul steam, and my full moon with waning, and my silver with tarnishing, and my rays with the dark.

Then said the boy, "The scorching of affliction be my lot rather than to take such an oath! let me yield to vengeance rather than swear as no one has ever sworn!" But the old man would naught but make him swallow the oath which he had framed for him, and the draughts which he had bittered. And the dispute ceased not to blaze between them, and the road of concord to be rugged. Now the boy, while thus resisting, captivated the Governor by his motions, and made him covet that he should belong to him; until love subdued his heart and fixed in his breast; and the passion which enslaved him, and the desire which he had imagined tempted him to liberate the boy and then get possession of him, to free him from the noose of the old man, and then catch him himself. So he said to the old man, "Hast thou a mind for that which is more seemly in the stronger and nearer to god-fearing?" He said, "Whither art thou pointing that I should follow and not delay?" He said, "I think it well that thou cease from altercation and be content with a hundred denars, on condition that I take on myself part of it, and collect the rest as may be." Said the old man, "I refuse not; but let there be no failure to thy promise." Then the Governor paid him down twenty and assigned among his attendants the making up of fifty. But the robe of evening grew dim, and from this cause the rain of collection was cut short. Then he said, "Take what is ready and leave disputing; and on me be it tomorrow to accomplish that the rest be doled to thee and reach thee." Said the old man, "I will do this on the condition that I keep close to him to-night, that the pupil of my eye guard him, until when on the dawning of the morn he has made up what remains of the sum of reconciliation, shell may get clear of chick, and he may go guiltless as the wolf went guiltless of the blood of the son of Jacob." Then said to him the Governor, "I think that thou dost not impose what is immoderate or ask what is excessive."

Said Al Harith, son of Hammam: Now when I perceived that the pleadings of the old man were as the pleadings of Ibn Surayj, I knew him to be the Glory of the Serujis: and I delayed until the stars of the darkness glittered, and the knots of the crowd dispersed: and then I sought the Governor's courtyard; and lo! the old man guarding the youth. And I adjured him by God to say whether he was Abu Zayd: he said, "Yes, by him who hath permitted the chase." I said, "Who is this boy, after whom the understanding darts?" He said, "In kin he is my chick, and in making gain my spring." I said, "Wilt thou not be satisfied with the graces of his make, and spare the Governor temptation by his forelock?" He said, "Were it not that his forehead put forth its ringlets, I should not have snatched the fifty." Then he said, "Pass the night near me that we may quench the fire of grief, and give enjoyment its turn after separation. For I have resolved to slip away at dawn, and to burn the Governor's heart with the flame of regret." Said Al Harith, Then I spent the night with him in conversation more pleasant than a garden of flowers, or a woodland of trees: until when the Wolf's Tail lighted the horizon, and the brightening of the daybreak came on in its time, he mounted the back of the highway, and left the Governor to taste burning torment. And he committed to me, in the hour of his departure a paper firmly closed, and said, "Hand it to the Governor when he has been bereft of composure, when he has convinced himself of our flight." But I broke the seal as one who would free himself from a letter of Mutelemmis, and behold there was written in it:

Tell the Governor whom I have left, after my departure, repenting, grieving, biting his hands,
That the old man has stolen his money and the young one his heart;
And he is scorched in the flame of a double regret.
He was generous with his coin when love blinded his eye, and he has ended with losing either.
Calm thy grief, O afflicted, for it profits not to seek the traces after the substance is gone.
But if what has befallen thee is terrible to thee as the ill-fate of Al Hosayn is terrible to the Moslems;
Yet hast thou gotten in exchange for it understanding and caution;
And the wise man, the prudent, wishes for these.
So henceforth resist desires, and know that the chasing of gazelles is not easy;
No, nor does every bird enter the springe, even though it be surrounded by silver.
And how many a one who seeks to make a prey becomes a prey himself,
And meets with naught but the shoes of Honayn!

Now consider well, and forecast not every thundercloud:
Many a thundercloud may have in it the bolts of death:
And cast down thine eye, that thou mayest rest from a passion
By which thou wouldest clothe thyself with the garment of infamy and disgrace.
For the trouble of man is the following of the soul's desire;
And the seed of desire is the longing look of the eye.

Said the narrator, But I tore the paper piecemeal, and cared not whether he blamed or pardoned me.

Al-Hariri Assemblies in Arab Literature

The Eleventh Assembly

Al Harith, son of Hammam, related: I was aware of hardness of heart while I sojourned at Saweh. So I betook myself to the Tradition handed down, that its cure is by visiting the tombs. And when I had reached the mansion of the dead, the storehouse of moldering remains, I saw an assemblage over a grave that had been dug, and a corpse that was being buried. So I drew aside to them, meditating on the end of man, and calling to mind those of my people who were gone. And when they had sepulchered the dead, and the crying of Alas! was over, an old man stood forth on high, from a hillock, leaning on a staff. And he had veiled his face with his cloak, and disguised his form for craftiness. And he said: Let those who work, work for an end like this. Now take thought, O yet negligent and gird yourselves, ye slothful, and look well, ye observers. How is it with you that the burying of your fellows grieves you not, and that the pouring in of the mold frightens you not; that ye heed not the visitations of misfortune; that ye prepare not for the going down to your graves; that ye are not moved to tears at the eye that weeps; that ye take not warning at the death-message when it is heard; that ye are not affrighted when an intimate is lost; that ye are not saddened when the mourning assembly is gathered. One of you follows home the dead man's bier, but his heart is set toward his house; and he is present at the burying of his kinsman, but his thought is of securing his portion. He leaves his loved friend with the worms, then retires alone with his pipes and lutes. Ye have sorrowed over your riches, if but a grain were notched away, yet have ye been forgetful of the cutting of of your friends: and ye have been cast down at the befalling of adversity, but have made little of the perishing of your kindred. Ye have laughed at a funeral as ye laughed not in the hour of dancing; ye have walked wantonly behind biers, as ye walked not in the day that ye grasped gifts. Ye have turned from the recital of the mourning women to the preparing of banquets; and from the anguish of the bereaved to daintiness in feastings. Ye care not for him who molders, and ye move not the thought of death in your mind. So that it is as if ye were joined to Death by clientship, or had gotten security from Time, or were confident of your own safety, or had made sure of a peace with the Destroyer of delights. No! it is an ill thing that ye imagine. Again, no! surely ye shall learn. Then he recited:

O thou who claimest understanding;
How long, O brother of delusion, wilt thou
marshal sin and blame, and err exceeding
error?
Is not the shame plain to thee?
Doth not hoariness warn thee? (and in its
counsel there is no doubtfulness);
Nor hath thy hearing become deaf.
Is not Death calling thee? doth he not make thee
hear his voice?
Dost thou not fear thy passing away, so as to be
wary and anxious?
How long wilt thou be bewildered in
carelessness, and walk proudly in vanity,
And go eagerly to diversion, as if death were not
for all?
'Till when will last thy swerving, and thy
delaying to mend habits that
Unite in thee vices whose every sort shall be
collected in thee?

If thou anger thy Master thou art not disquieted at it;
But if thy scheme be bootless thou burnest with vexation.
If the graving of the yellow one gleam to thee thou art joyful;
But if the bier pass by thee thou feignest grief, and there is no grief.
Thou resistest him who counseleth righteousness;
Thou art hard in understanding;
Thou swervest aside: but thou followest the guiding of him who deceiveth, who lieth, who defameth.
Thou walkest in the desire of thy soul;
Thou schemest after money;
But thou forgettest the darkness of the grave, and rememberest not what is there.
But if true happiness had looked upon thee, thy own look would not have led thee amiss;
Nor wouldest thou be saddened when the preaching wipeth away griefs.
Thou shalt weep blood, not tears, when thou perceivest that no company
Can protect thee in the Court of Assembling; no kinsman of mother or father.
It is as though I could see thee when thou goest down to the vault and divest deep;
When thy kinsmen have committed thee to a

place narrower than a needle's eye.
There is the body stretched out that the worms may devour it,
Until the coffin-wood is bored through and the bones molder.
And afterward there is no escape from that review of souls:
Since Sirat is prepared; its bridge is stretched over the fire to every one who cometh thither.
And how many a guide shall go astray! and how many a great one shall be vile!
And how many a learned one shall slip and say, "The business surpasseth."
Therefore hasten, O simple one, to that by which the bitter is made sweet;
For thy life is now near to decay and thou hast not withdrawn thyself from blame.
And rely not on fortune though it be soft, though it be gay:
For so wilt thou be found like one deceived by a viper that spitteth venom.
And lower thyself from thy loftiness;
For death is meeting thee and reaching at thy collar;
And he is one who shrinketh not back when he hath purposed.
And avoid proud turning away of the cheek if fortune have prospered thee:
Bridle thy speech if it would run astray; for how

happy is he who bridleth it!
And relieve the brother of sorrow, and believe
him when he speaketh and mend thy ragged
conduct; For he hath prospered who mendeth it.
And plume him whose plumage hath fallen in
calamity great or small;
And sorrow not at the loss, and be not covetous
in amassing.
And resist thy base nature, and accustom thy
hand to liberality
And listen not to blame for it, and keep thy hand
from hoarding
And make provision of good for thy soul, and
leave that which will bring on ill,
And prepare the ship for thy journey, and dread
the deep of the sea.
Thus have I given my precepts, friends, and
shown as one who showeth clearly:
And happy the man who walketh by my
doctrines and maketh them his example.

Then he drew back his sleeve from an arm strong of sinew, on which he had fastened the splints of deceit not of fracture; presenting himself to beg in the garb of impudence: and by it he beguiled those people until his sleeve was brimmed and full; then he came down from the hillock merry at the gift. Said the narrator: But I pulled him from behind by the hem of his cloak;

and he turned to me submissively, and faced me, saluting me: and lo! it was our old Abu Zayd, in his very self, and in all his deceit: and I said to him, *How many, Abu Zayd, will be the varieties of thy cunning to drive the prey to thy net? and wilt thou not care who censures?* And he answered without shame and without hesitation: *Look well, and leave thy blaming; for, tell me, hast thou ever known a time when a man would not win of the world when the game was in his hands?*

Then I said to him: Away with thee, Old Shaykh of Hell, laden with infamy! For there is nothing like thee for the fairness of thy seeming and the foulness of thy purpose; except silvered dung or a whited sewer. Then we parted; and I went away to the right, and he went away to the left; and I set myself to the quarter of the south, and he set himself to the quarter of the north.

Al-Hariri Assemblies in Arab Literature

The Twelfth Assembly

Al Harith, son of Hammam, related: I journeyed from Iraq to the Ghutah; and then was I master of haltered steeds and envied wealth. Freedom of arm called me to diversion, fullness of store led me to pride. And when I had reached the place after toil of soul, after making lean my camel, I found it such as tongues describe it; and in it was whatever souls long for or eyes delight in. So I thanked the bounty of travel and ran a heat with pleasure: and began there to break the seals of desires and gather the clusters of delights, until some travelers were making ready for the journey to Iraq, and I had so recovered from my drowning, that regret visited me in calling to mind my home and longing after my fold. Then I struck the tents of exile and saddled the steeds of return. And when the company had equipped themselves and agreement was completed, we shrank from setting forth without taking with us a guard. And we sought one from every tribe and used a thousand devices to obtain him. But to find him in the clans failed, so that we thought he was not among the living. And for the want of such a one the resolves of the travelers were bewildered, and they assembled at the gate of Jayrun to take counsel. And they ceased not tying and untying, and plaiting and twining, until suggestion was exhausted and the hoper despaired. But opposite them was a person whose demeanor was as the demeanor of the youthful, and his garb as the garb of monks, and in his hand was the rosary of women, and in his eyes the mark of giddiness from watchings. And he had fastened his gaze on the assemblage and sharpened his ear to steal a hearing. And when it was the time of their turning homeward and their secret was manifest to him, he said to them, "O people, let your care relieve itself, let your mind be tranquil; for I will guard you with that which shall put off your fear and show itself in accord with you." Said the narrator: Then we asked him to show us concerning his safe conduct, and promised him a higher wage for it than for an embassy. And he declared it to be some words which he had been taught in a dream, whereby to guard himself from the malice of mankind. Then began one to steal a look at another, and to move his eyes between glances sideward and downward. So that it was plain to him that we thought meanly of his story, and conceived it to be futile. Whereupon he said, How is it that ye take my earnest for jest, and treat my gold as dross? Now, by Allah, oft have I gone through fearful tracts and entered among deadly dangers: and with this I have needed not the companying of a guard or to take with me a quiver. Besides, I will remove what gives you doubt, I will draw away the distrust that has come on you, in that I will consent with you in the desert and accompany you on the Semaweh. Then, if my promise has spoken you true, do ye renew my weal and prosper my fortune: but if my mouth has lied to you, then rend my skin and pour out my blood.

Said Al Harith, son of Hammam: Then we were inspired to believe his vision and take as true what he had related; so we ceased from disputing with him and cast lots for carrying him. And at his word we cut the loops of hindrance, and put away fear of harm or stay; and when the pack-saddles were fastened on and the setting forth was near, we sought to learn from him the magic words that we might make them a lasting safeguard. He said: "Let each of you repeat the Mother of the Qur'an as often as day or night comes on; then let him say with lowly tongue and humble voice: O God! O thou who givest life to the moldering dead! O thou who avertest harms! O thou who guardest from terrors! O thou generous in rewarding! O thou the refuge of suppliants! O thou the Lord of pardon and protection! Send thy blessing on Mohammed, the Seal of thy prophets, the Bringer of thy messages, and on the Lights of his kindred, the Keys of his victory; and give me refuge, O God, from the mischiefs of devils and the assaults of princes; from the vexing of the wrongers, and from suffering through the tyrannous; from the enmity of transgressors, and from the transgression of enemies; from the conquest of conquerors, from the spoiling of spoilers, from the crafts of the crafty, from the treacheries of the treacherous; and deliver me, O God, from the wrongfulness of neighbors and the neighborhood of the wrongful; and keep from me the hands of the harmful; bring me forth from the darkness of the oppressors; place me by thy mercy among thy servants who do aright. O God, keep me in my own land and in my journeying, in my exile and my coming homeward, in my foraging and my return from it, in my trafficking and my success from it, in my adventuring and my withdrawing from it. And guard me in myself and my property, in my honor and my goods, in my family and my means, in my household and my dwelling, in my strength and my fortune, in my riches and my death. Bring not on me reverse; make not the invader lord over me, but give me from thyself helping power. O God, watch over me with thy eye and thy aid, distinguish me by thy safeguard and thy bounty, befriend me with thy election and thy good, and consign me not to the keeping of any but thee. But grant to me health that weareth not away, and allot to me comfort that perisheth not; and free me from the terrors of misfortune, and shelter me with the coverings of thy boons; make not the talons of enemies to prevail against me, for thou art he that heareth prayer."

Then he looked down, and he turned not a glance, he answered not a word: so that we said, "A fear has confounded him or a stupor struck him dumb." Then he raised his head and drew his breath, and said, "I swear by the heaven with its constellations, and the earth with its plains, and the pouring flood, and the blazing sun, and the sounding sea, and the wind and the dust-storm, that this is the most sure of charms, one that will best suffice you for the wearers of the helmet. He who repeats it at the smiling of the dawn has no alarm of danger to the red of eve; and he who whispers it to the vanguard of the dark is safe the night long from plunder."

Said the narrator: So we learned it till we knew it thoroughly, and rehearsed it together that we might not forget it. Then we set forth, urging the beasts by prayers, not by the song of drivers; and guarding the loads by words, not by warriors. And our companion frequented us evening and morning, but required not of us our promises: 'till when we spied the house-tops of 'Anah, he said to us, "Now, your help, your help!" Then we set before him the exposed and the hidden, and showed him the corded and the sealed, and said to him, "Decide as thou wilt, for thou wilt find among us none but will consent." But nothing enlivened him but the light, the adorning; nothing was comely in his eye but the coin. So of those he loaded on his burden, and rose up with enough to repair his poverty. Then he dodged us as dodges the cutpurse, and slipped away from us as slips quicksilver. And his departure saddened us, his shooting away astonished us: and we ceased not to seek him in every assembly, and to ask news of him from each that might mislead or guide. Until it was said, "Since he entered 'Anah he has not quitted the tavern." Then the foulness of this report set me on to test it, and to walk in a path to which I belonged not. So I went by night to the wine-hall in disguised habit; and there was the old man in a gay-colored dress amid casks and wine-vats; and about him were cup-bearers surpassing in beauty, and lights that glittered, and the myrtle and the jasmine, and the pipe and the lute. And at one time he bade broach the wine-casks, and at another he called the lutes to give utterance; and now he inhaled the perfumes, and now he courted the gazelles. But when I had thus stumbled on his hypocrisy, and the differing of his today from his yesterday, I said to him, Woe to thee, accursed! hast thou forgotten the day at the Jayrun? But he laughed heartily, and then indited charmingly:

I cling to journeying, I cross deserts, I loathe pride that I may cull joy:
And I plunge into floods, and tame steeds that I may draw the trains of pleasure and delight.
And I throw away staidness, and sell my land, for the sipping of wine, for the quaffing of cups.
And were it not for longing after the drinking of wine my mouth would not utter its elegancies
Nor would my craft have lured the travelers to the land of Iraq, through my carrying of

rosaries.
Now be not angry, nor cry aloud, nor chide, for my excuse is plain:
And wonder not at an old man who settles himself in a well-filled house
By a wine-cask that is brimming.
For truly wine strengthens the bones and heals sickness and drives away grief.
And the purest of joy is when the grave man throws off the veils of shame and flings them aside:
And the sweetest of passion is when the love-crazed ceases from the concealing of his love,
And shows it openly.
Then avow thy love and cool thy heart: or else the fire-staff of thy grief will rub a spark on it;
And heal thy wounds, and draw out thy cares by the daughter of the vine, her the desired:
And assign to thy evening draught a cup-bearer who will stir the torment of desire when she gazes;
And a singer who will raise such a voice that the mountains of iron shall thrill at it when she chants.
And rebel against the adviser who will not permit thee to approach a beauty when she consents.
And range in thy cunning even to perverseness; and care not what is said of thee,

And catch what suits thee:
And leave thy father if he refuse thee, and spread thy nets and hunt who comes by thee.
But be sincere with thy friend, and avoid the niggardly, and bestow kindness,
And be constant in gifts;
And take refuge in repentance before thy departure;
For whoso knocks at the door of the Merciful causes it to open.

Then I said to him, "O rare thy recitation, but fie on thy misconduct! Now, by Allah, tell me from what thicket is thy root, for thy puzzle vexes me." He said I love not to disclose myself; yet I will intimate it:

I am the novelty of the time, the wonder of nations
I am the wily one, who plays his wiles among Arabs and foreigners
But not the less a brother of need, whom fortune vexes and wrongs
And the father of children who lie out like meat on the tray:
Now the brother of want, who has a household, is not blamed if he be wily.

Said the narrator: Then I knew that it was Abu Zayd, the man of ill-fame and disgrace, he that blackens the face of his hoariness. And the greatness of his contumacy offended me, and the foulness of the path of his resorting: so I said to him with the tongue of indignation and the confidence of acquaintance: "Is it not time, old man, that thou withdraw from debauchery?" But he was angry, and growled, and his countenance changed, and he thought a while: and then he said, "It is a night for merriment, not for rebuke, an occasion for drinking wine, not for contention; so leave speaking thy thought until we meet tomorrow." Then I left him, through fear of his drunken humor, not through dependence on his promise; and I passed my night clothed in the mourning of repentance, at having advanced the steps of my foot to the daughter of the vine, not of grace. And I made a vow to God Almighty that I would never again enter the tavern of a liquor-seller, even that I might be endowed with the dominion of Baghdad; and that I would not look upon the vats of wine, even that the season of youth might be restored to me. Then we saddled the white camels in the last darkness of night, and left together Abu Zayd and Iblis.

Sources:

Nicholson,R.A. *A Literary History of the Arabs*, Cambridge University Press, 1977,PP.328-335.

From: Charles F. Horne, ed., *The Sacred Books and Early Literature of the East,* (New York: Parke, Austin, & Lipscomb, 1917), Vol. VI: *Medieval Arabia*, pp. 143-201.

There are fify *maqamat* (assemblies) by al-Hariri (aka Kasim ibn `Ali). Twelve of these are reprinted in the Sacred Books of the East volume.

Scanned by Jerome S. Arkenberg, Cal. State Fullerton. The text has been modernized by Prof. Arkenberg.

This text is part of the Internet Medieval Source Book. The Sourcebook is a collection of public domain and copy-permitted texts related to medieval and Byzantine history.

About the Editors

Sheila J. Summerfield is a British Journalist at the BBC Inc., Australia. She earned her degree from Cambridge University and works as international correspondent at the International media Agency, Chicago. She published several books on Aesop Fables and al-Hariri .Assembles. (Maqamat).

Hasan A. Yahya is an Arab American scholar, a professor of sociology. He earned his degrees from AU Beirut Lebanon and Michigan State University. He works as judge consultant for education and social policies. He is also a poet, and writer. He published over than 90 books and several hundreds of articles.